I0448818

July 2013

FLOOD INSURANCE

Implications of Changing Coverage Limits and Expanding Coverage

GAO-13-568

GAO Highlights

Highlights of GAO-13-568, a report to congressional committees

July 2013

FLOOD INSURANCE

Implications of Changing Coverage Limits and Expanding Coverage

Why GAO Did This Study

NFIP was created in 1968 and is the only federal flood insurance available. It may be the sole source of insurance to some residents of flood-prone areas. Mainly due to catastrophic losses in 2005, the program became indebted to the U.S. Treasury and has been unable to repay this debt. Because of NFIP's financial instability and management challenges, GAO placed the program on its High-Risk List in 2006. The Biggert-Waters Flood Insurance Reform Act of 2012 introduced many changes to the program and mandates GAO to study the effects of increasing the maximum coverage limits ($250,000 for residential buildings and $500,000 for commercial buildings) and providing optional coverage for business interruption and additional living expenses. This report discusses (1) existing flood insurance coverage, (2) the potential effects of changing NFIP coverage limits, and (3) the potential effects of allowing NFIP to offer optional coverage for business interruption and additional living expenses. To address these objectives, GAO analyzed data from NFIP's databases of policies and claims, reviewed prior reports, and interviewed brokers, insurers, and representatives from consumer advocacy and industry organizations.

What GAO Recommends

GAO continues to support previous recommendations to the Federal Emergency Management Agency (FEMA) that address the need to ensure that the methods and data used to set NFIP rates accurately reflect the risk of losses from flooding. FEMA agreed and has taken some steps to begin to implement them.

View GAO-13-568. For more information, contact Alicia Puente Cackley, 202-512-8678, or cackleya@gao.gov.

What GAO Found

The National Flood Insurance Program (NFIP) currently has more than 5.5 million policyholders insured for about $1.3 trillion who pay about $3.5 billion in annual premiums, but less than half purchase maximum coverage—a possible indicator of how many might purchase additional coverage were it offered. However, from 2002 through 2012, the proportion of residential and commercial policies at maximum building coverage rose substantially—from 11 to 42 percent and from 21 to 36 percent, respectively. States along the Gulf and East Coasts have the most residential policyholders with maximum coverage. In addition, states with higher median home values generally have a higher percentage of policyholders purchasing coverage up to the limit. Industry stakeholders said that an unknown number of policyholders with higher-value properties choose to purchase additional, or excess, coverage above the NFIP limit through the private flood insurance market—a small and selective group of insurers.

Percentage of Residential Single-Unit and Commercial Policyholders with Maximum Building Coverage, as of September 2012

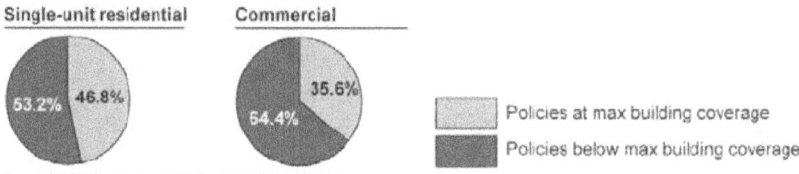

Single-unit residential: 53.2%, 46.8%
Commercial: 64.4%, 35.6%

Policies at max building coverage
Policies below max building coverage

Source: GAO analysis of NFIP's Database of Policies

Increasing coverage limits could increase the net revenue of the program and have varying effects on NFIP, the private insurance market, and consumers. Assuming that higher coverage limits had been in effect from 2002 through 2011, GAO's analysis suggests that NFIP still would have suffered losses during years with catastrophic floods, such as 2004 and 2005, but would have experienced net increases in revenue in other years. Such increases could have offset future losses or helped avoid additional debt, but the overall financial impact and risk to the program would depend on the adequacy of the rates charged, which GAO has questioned in the past, and the number of policyholders opting for additional coverage. Regarding the private flood insurance market and consumers, higher NFIP coverage limits could decrease participating insurers' overall risk exposure and provide more options to consumers, but might lessen participation of private insurers, as consumers might need to purchase less private insurance.

Adding optional coverage to NFIP for business interruption and additional living expenses could result in less uninsured risk in the market, but further negatively impact the financial stability of the program. Industry stakeholders told GAO that business interruption coverage is generally purchased by only larger companies, as its high cost prohibits small- and medium-sized companies from being able to afford it. In addition, adding business interruption coverage to NFIP could be particularly challenging. For example, properly pricing risk, underwriting, and claim processing can be complex. NFIP officials have stated that they would have to hire additional expertise in-house to offer this coverage. Similarly, offering optional coverage for additional living expenses has many of the same potential effects on NFIP, the private market, and consumers, although this coverage is generally less complex to administer.

_____ United States Government Accountability Office

Contents

Abbreviations

FEMA	Federal Emergency Management Agency
FIRM	Flood Insurance Rate Map
HUD	Department of Housing and Urban Development
NFIP	National Flood Insurance Program
SFHA	Special Flood Hazard Area
WYO	Write-Your-Own

GAO

U.S. GOVERNMENT ACCOUNTABILITY OFFICE

441 G St. N.W.
Washington, DC 20548

July 3, 2013

The Honorable Tim Johnson
Chairman
The Honorable Mike Crapo
Ranking Member
Committee on Banking, Housing and Urban Affairs
United States Senate

The Honorable Jeb Hensarling
Chairman
The Honorable Maxine Waters
Ranking Member
Committee on Financial Services
House of Representatives

The National Flood Insurance Program (NFIP) is a key component of the federal government's efforts to minimize the damage and financial impact of floods and is the only source of insurance against flood damage for most residents of flood-prone areas. NFIP is administered by the Federal Emergency Management Agency (FEMA) within the Department of Homeland Security and was created in 1968. As of the end of fiscal year 2012, the program had more than 5.5 million policies insured for about $1.3 trillion that paid about $3.5 billion in annual premiums.

Until 2004, NFIP was able to cover most of its claims with premiums it collected and occasional loans from the U.S. Treasury (Treasury) that it repaid. However, after the 2005 hurricanes—primarily Hurricane Katrina—the program borrowed $16.8 billion from Treasury to cover the unprecedented number of claims. NFIP has since received additional borrowing authority in the amount of $9.7 billion to cover claims for Superstorm Sandy—and as of May 2013, it owed approximately $24 billion.[1]

Prior to the Biggert-Waters Flood Insurance Reform Act of 2012 (Biggert-Waters Act), structural weaknesses in the way the program was funded

---

[1]Pub. L. No. 113-1, 127 Stat. 3 (Jan. 6, 2013). In addition to the amounts borrowed to pay claims, Treasury charges FEMA interest on the outstanding debt.

and operated made it unlikely that NFIP would be able to repay its debt in the near future.[2] However, the act reauthorized the program through 2017 and made some significant changes, such as eliminating the subsidies for certain properties, creating a reserve fund, and eliminating the grandfathering of properties to old rates after remapping. Because most of these reforms are being phased in over time, their final financial impact on the program remains unknown.

As a result of the program's importance, level of indebtedness, potential for future losses, and management challenges, we placed NFIP on our High-Risk List in March 2006.[3] Although the Biggert-Waters Act addressed some of NFIP's structural weaknesses and may help increase NFIP's long-term financial stability, the program still faces challenges and the ultimate effect of the changes is not yet known. In earlier reports, we identified a number of operational challenges that hindered FEMA's ability to effectively administer NFIP and contributed to NFIP's placement on the list.[4] Any efforts to help stabilize NFIP will require addressing both the program's financial challenges and its operational and management issues.

The Biggert-Waters Act included several mandates for GAO studies, two of which are addressed in this report.[5] Specifically, the act mandated that GAO study the impact of increasing the maximum amount of coverage available under an NFIP policy and the impact of NFIP providing optional coverage for business interruption and additional living expenses. This report discusses (1) existing federal flood insurance coverage, (2) the potential effects on NFIP's financial condition, the private insurance market, and consumers of raising or lowering NFIP coverage limits, and (3) the potential effects on NFIP's financial condition, the private insurance market, and consumers of allowing NFIP to offer optional coverage for business interruption and additional living expenses.

---

[2]Pub. L. No. 112-141, Title II, Sub. A, 126 Stat. 405, 916 (July 6, 2012).

[3]GAO, *GAO's High-Risk Program*, GAO-06-497T (Washington, D.C.: Mar. 15, 2006).

[4]GAO, *Flood Insurance: FEMA's Rate-Setting Process Warrants Attention*, GAO-09-12 (Washington, D.C.: Oct. 31, 2008); *FEMA: Action Needed to Improve Administration of the National Flood Insurance Program*, GAO-11-297 (Washington, D.C.: June 9, 2011); and *High-Risk Series: An Update*, GAO-13-283 (Washington, D.C.: February 2013).

[5]Pub. L. No. 112-141, Title II, Sub. A, §§100231(a), 100233, 126 Stat. 405, 949, 955 (July 6, 2012).

To describe the existing federal flood insurance market, we analyzed NFIP's Policy and Claims Masterfiles. We used NFIP's database of policies to identify all residential single-unit and nonresidential (commercial) claims with maximum coverage at the end of fiscal year 2012.[6] We also analyzed the policy database to identify the total residential policies and commercial policies for each fiscal year from 2002 through 2012 and calculated the proportional increase of those with maximum building coverage. We further analyzed residential single-unit policy coverage for 2011 to investigate the association between the percentage of each state's policyholders with maximum coverage and a state's median home value. In addition, we calculated average payments for residential and commercial claims that were closed and closed without payment for the period from 2007 through 2012 using data from FEMA's BureauNet.[7] To address the effect on NFIP, the private insurance market, and consumers of increasing NFIP coverage limits or adding optional coverage for business interruption and additional living expenses, we interviewed industry experts, including representatives from FEMA, insurance industry organizations, brokers, insurance companies, and consumer advocacy organizations. Using NFIP's claims and policy databases, we estimated the effect on NFIP's financial condition of raising coverage limits from $250,000 to $417,000 by estimating the impact on net revenue (premiums less claim payments) for residential single-unit dwellings from 2002 through 2011.[8] We conducted electronic testing of specific data elements to test for missing data, validity, and reasonableness and interviewed knowledgeable agency officials to assure the reliability of the data, and we determined the data to be reliable for our purposes. To address all objectives, we also reviewed prior GAO reports and testimonies and relevant studies conducted by

---

[6]Nonresidential includes, but is not limited to, small businesses, churches, schools, farm buildings (including grain bins and silos), pool houses, clubhouses, recreational buildings, mercantile structures, agricultural and industrial structures, warehouses, hotels and motels with normal room rentals for less than 6 months' duration, and nursing homes. For the purposes of this report, we refer to nonresidential policies as commercial.

[7]BureauNet is the system that FEMA uses to collect, manage, and access its policy, claims, and policyholder data.

[8]The upper limit of $417,000 used in our analysis, as required by the Biggert-Waters Act, corresponds to the conforming loan limit for Fannie Mae and Freddie Mac (the enterprises). The enterprises are restricted by law to purchasing single-family mortgages with origination balances below a specific amount, known as the "conforming loan limit." The limit was increased to $417,000 in 2006 and remained at this level, as of 2012, with exceptions for certain high-cost areas.

RAND, Wharton Risk Management and Decision Processes Center, Deloitte Consulting LLP, the Congressional Research Service, and academia. For more information on our scope and methodology, see appendix I.

We conducted this performance audit from September 2012 to July 2013 in accordance with generally accepted government auditing standards. Those standards require that we plan and perform the audit to obtain sufficient, appropriate evidence to provide a reasonable basis for our findings and conclusions based on our audit objectives. We believe that the evidence obtained provides a reasonable basis for our findings and conclusions based on our audit objectives.

Background

History of NFIP

The National Flood Insurance Act of 1968 established NFIP as an alternative to providing direct disaster relief after floods.[9] NFIP, which makes federally backed flood insurance available to residential property owners and businesses, was intended to reduce the federal government's escalating costs for repairing flood damage after disasters. Floods are the most common and destructive natural disaster in the United States. However, flooding is generally excluded from homeowners' insurance policies that typically cover damages from other losses, such as wind, fire, and theft. Because of the catastrophic nature of flooding and the inability to adequately predict flood risks, private insurance companies have historically been largely unwilling to underwrite and bear the risk that results from providing primary flood insurance coverage. Under NFIP, the federal government currently assumes the liability for the insurance coverage and sets rates and coverage limitations, among other responsibilities, while the private insurance industry sells the policies and administers the claims for a fee determined by FEMA. Some of these same insurers also provide coverage for flood insurance above the limit of NFIP coverage. A number of private insurers that do not sell and administer NFIP policies also offer flood insurance. Flood insurance purchased above current NFIP coverage limits generally is referred to as excess flood insurance.

---

[9]Pub. L. No. 90-448, Title XIII, § 1302, 82 Stat. 476, 572 (Aug. 1, 1968).

Since NFIP's inception, Congress has several times enacted legislation to strengthen certain aspects of the program. The Flood Disaster Protection Act of 1973 made flood insurance mandatory for owners of properties in vulnerable areas who had mortgages from federally insured or regulated lenders.[10] The act also provided additional incentives for communities to join the program. Community participation in NFIP is voluntary. However, communities must join NFIP and adopt FEMA-approved building standards and floodplain management strategies in order for their residents to purchase flood insurance through the program. The National Flood Insurance Reform Act of 1994 strengthened the mandatory purchase requirement for federally backed mortgages of properties located in special flood hazard areas (SFHA).[11] The Bunning-Bereuter-Blumenauer Flood Insurance Reform Act of 2004 established a pilot program to encourage owners of properties that continually suffer from repeated flood losses to take steps to reduce the risk of damage, known as mitigation.[12] Owners of these "repetitive loss" properties who do not mitigate the risks face higher premiums.[13] Finally, the Biggert-Waters Act reauthorized the program through 2017 and removed subsidized rates for a number of insured properties, such as residential property that is not the primary residence, severe repetitive loss properties, business properties, and property that has incurred flood-related damage for which the cumulative amounts of payments equaled or exceeded the fair market value of the property.

Premiums

NFIP studies and maps flood risks, assigning flood zone designations based on the risk level for flooding. The type of NFIP policy and the subsequent rate a policyholder pays depend on several property

---

[10]Pub. L. No. 93-234, Title I, §102, 87 Stat. 975, 979 (Dec. 31, 1973).

[11]Pub. L. No. 103-325, Title V, 108 Stat. 2160 (Sept. 23, 1994).

[12]Pub. L. No. 108-264, Title I, § 102, 118 Stat. 712 (June 30, 2004). According to FEMA, the key mitigation steps for residential properties are elevating a building to or above the area's base flood elevation, relocating the building to an area of less flood risk, or demolishing the building and turning the property into green space. A community can also take steps to reduce flood risk to an area by diverting the flow of water through well-designed channels and retaining walls or by containing the water through ponds and green space.

[13]Generally, repetitive loss properties are those that have either four or more claims exceeding $5,000 each with a cumulative payment amount over $20,000 or two claims with a cumulative payment amount exceeding the value of the property.

characteristics. For example, whether the building was built before or after the development of the community's Flood Insurance Rate Map (FIRM) and where the building is located relative to the floodplain—the flood zone—can affect the type of policy and rate available to a policyholder. Flood insurance rates are calculated for each flood zone.[14] Areas that have a 1-percent chance of flooding in a given year are at high risk for flooding and are generally referred to as SFHAs.[15] These areas are designated as zones A or V (see table 1). Areas designated as V or VE are located along the coast. Areas with moderate to low risk for flooding are designated as zones B, C, or X.

Table 1: NFIP Flood Zone Designations

Designations	Risk level
Flood zones B, C, X	Moderate to low risk
Flood zones A, AE	High risk
Flood zones V, VE	High-risk coastal
Flood zone D	Undetermined risk

Source: FEMA.

NFIP offers two types of flood insurance premiums to property owners who live in participating communities: subsidized and full-risk. The National Flood Insurance Act of 1968 authorized NFIP to offer subsidized premiums to owners of certain properties. These subsidized rates are not based on flood risk and, according to FEMA, represent only about 40 to 45 percent of the full flood risk. Congress originally mandated the use of subsidized premiums to encourage communities to join the program and mitigate concerns that charging rates that fully and accurately reflected flood risk would be a burden to some property owners. According to FEMA, Congress made changes to the program over the years to encourage further participation in NFIP through low premiums. However, as mentioned previously, the Biggert-Waters Act eliminated the existing subsidies for certain types of properties.

---

[14]Various other factors such as structure elevation, type of structure, and amount of coverage also affect the premiums.

[15]SFHAs, which are depicted on NFIP maps, represent the land area that would be submerged by the floodwaters of the "base," or 1 percent annual chance of flood. FEMA commonly refers to this type of flood as the 100-year floodplain, however, the 100-year flood is not a flood that occurs every 100 years.

Differences from Private Insurers

The insurance operations of NFIP differ from those of most private insurers in a number of ways. For example, by design NFIP does not operate for profit like a private insurer but must instead meet a public policy goal—to provide flood insurance in flood-prone areas to property owners who otherwise would not be able to obtain it. At the same time, it is expected to cover its claims losses and operating expenses with the premiums it collects, much like private insurers. In years when flooding has not been catastrophic, NFIP has generally managed to meet these competing goals. But in years of catastrophic flooding, such as 2005, it has not done so and has exercised its authority to borrow from Treasury to pay claims. This arrangement results in much of the financial risk of flooding being transferred to the federal government and ultimately the taxpayer. Further, unlike private insurers that generally are not subject to limits on premium rate increases, FEMA is limited in how much it can raise rates. Prior to passage of the Biggert-Waters Act, FEMA had been prevented from raising rates on each flood zone by more than 10 percent each year, although the act now allows rate increases of up to 20 percent.[16] The Biggert-Waters Act further changed the program when it eliminated subsidies for certain properties, such as severe repetitive loss properties and properties for which the policyholders let their flood insurance lapse.

NFIP is also required to accept virtually all applications for insurance and cannot deny coverage or increase premium rates based on the frequency of losses. Private insurers, on the other hand, may reject applicants or increase rates if they believe the risk of loss is too high. As a result, NFIP is less able to offset the effects of adverse selection—the phenomenon that those who are most likely to purchase insurance are also the most likely to experience losses.[17] Adverse selection may also lead to a concentration of policyholders in the riskiest areas. This problem is further compounded when those policyholders with properties at greatest risk are required to purchase insurance from NFIP because they have a mortgage from a federally insured or regulated lender.

---

[16] Pub. L. No. 112-141, § 100205(c)(2), 126 Stat. 918.

[17] Adverse selection occurs when insurers cannot distinguish between less risky and more risky properties, although homeowners can. When premiums do not reflect differences in risk that are known to potential policyholders, those who buy insurance are often those at greatest risk for the hazards covered. Adverse selection in the market for natural catastrophe insurance suggests that homeowners who are at the highest risk of experiencing a natural catastrophe will buy available insurance.

Role of Write-Your-Own Insurance Companies

Since its inception, NFIP, to a large extent, has relied on the private insurance industry to sell and service policies, and in 1983, FEMA established the Write-Your-Own (WYO) program.[18] Private insurers become WYOs by entering into an arrangement with FEMA to issue flood policies in their own name. WYOs adjust flood claims and settle, pay, and defend all claims arising from the flood policies but assume no flood risk. Insurance agents from these companies are the main point of contact for most policyholders. Based on information the insurance agents submit, WYOs issue policies, collect premiums, deduct an allowance for commission and operating expenses from the premiums, and remit the balance to NFIP. In most cases, insurance companies hire subcontractors—flood insurance vendors—to conduct some or all of the day-to-day processing and management of flood insurance policies. When flood losses occur, policyholders report them to their insurance agents, who notify the WYO insurance companies. The WYO companies review the claims and process approved claims for payment. FEMA reimburses the WYO insurance companies for the amount of the claims plus expenses for adjusting and processing the claims, using rates that FEMA establishes.

The WYO program was established to increase the NFIP policy base and the geographic distribution of policies, improve service to NFIP policyholders through the infusion of insurance industry knowledge, and provide the insurance industry with direct operating experience with flood insurance. In the first year of the WYO program, 48 WYO insurance companies were responsible for about 50 percent of the more than 2 million policies in force. As of September 2012, about 85 WYO insurance companies accounted for about 85 percent of the more than 5.5 million policies in force.[19]

---

[18]From 1969 through 1977, the Department of Housing and Urban Development (HUD), which administered NFIP at the time, had an agreement with a consortium of private insurers known as the National Flood Insurers Association. Under this agreement, HUD reimbursed the association for operating costs and provided an annual operating allowance equal to 5 percent of policyholders' premiums. From 1978 to 1983, a federal contractor—not an insurance company—sold and serviced policies.

[19]Although WYOs handle most flood policies, FEMA still contracts with a company that serves as the insurer of last resort when an eligible customer cannot purchase insurance-- including standard policies and others, such as repetitive loss and group policies--from a WYO.

Policy Coverage

Potential policyholders can purchase flood insurance to cover both buildings and contents for residential and commercial properties. NFIP's maximum coverage limit for residential policyholders is $250,000 per unit for building property and $100,000 per unit for contents. This coverage includes replacement value of the building and its foundation, electrical and plumbing systems, central air and heating, furnaces and water heater, and equipment considered part of the overall structure of the building. Personal property coverage includes items such as clothing, furniture, and portable electronic equipment. For commercial policyholders, the maximum coverage is $500,000 per unit for buildings and $500,000 for contents. Commercial coverage is similar to residential with regard to what is covered.

NFIP policies do not provide coverage for business interruption or additional living expenses, which currently are available through some private insurers. Private coverage for business interruption generally includes the loss of income that a business sustains after a disaster while the business is closed for repairs, as well as temporary relocation expenses and ongoing expenses to sustain the business, such as payroll and rent. To obtain coverage for business interruption for a loss caused by flood, the commercial customer must purchase excess flood insurance coverage from a private insurance company. Private coverage for additional living expenses generally includes the expenses for living outside of the home when the home has been damaged due to a covered peril.[20] It only includes expenses above normal living expenses, such as those required to maintain the household's normal standard of living if the family must live elsewhere until the dwelling has been repaired. Expenses typically include rent for a temporary rental home or hotel room, the extra cost of dining at restaurants compared to normal groceries, laundry, extra transportation costs to and from work or school, relocation and storage expenses, and furniture rental for a temporary residence. Generally, coverage for additional living expenses is automatically included in the standard homeowners' policy, but the standard homeowners' policy excludes coverage for these types of expenses when the losses result from flooding.

---

[20]According to FEMA, while most homeowner policies include coverage for additional living expenses, it only includes perils included in their policy—generally fires, hail, wind storms, and others, but not floods.

Less Than Half of Policyholders Purchase Maximum Coverage from NFIP for Buildings and Contents

Our analysis of NFIP's database of policies showed that fewer than half of all residential and commercial policyholders had maximum flood coverage for buildings, a possible indicator of how many policyholders might purchase additional coverage if the limits were increased. As of September 30, 2012, our analysis showed a total of 4,126,802 residential single-unit policies in force.[21] Of these, 46.8 percent (1,931,958) had purchased the maximum flood insurance coverage of $250,000 for buildings, 33 percent (1,363,367) had purchased the maximum coverage of $100,000 for contents, and 31.7 percent (1,307,734) had purchased maximum coverage for both buildings and contents. As of September 30, 2012, our analysis also showed a total of 283,398 commercial policies in the NFIP policy database. Of these, 35.6 percent (100,975) had purchased maximum coverage of $500,000 for buildings, and 10.9 percent (30,839) had purchased maximum coverage of $500,000 for contents. The percentage of commercial policyholders who purchased maximum coverage for both buildings and contents was 8.3 percent (23,507).

As NFIP has grown and the total number of residential and commercial policies has increased over time, the percentage of all residential and commercial policies that carried maximum coverage has also increased. We found that residential policies at maximum building limits increased from 11 percent in 2002 to 42 percent in 2012, as shown in figure 1.[22] Similarly, the proportion of commercial policies at maximum building coverage also increased during this period—from 21 percent in 2002 to 36 percent in 2012. According to FEMA officials, the primary reason for the increased proportion of policies purchased at maximum limits is the increase in the value of real estate. The average claim amount was much lower than the maximum coverage limit. The average residential flood claim from 2007 through 2012 was $31,020, and the average commercial claim was $66,176 for the same period.[23] According to FEMA officials, these average claim amounts have generally remained stable since 2002 except in catastrophic years, such as 2005. Because these are

---

[21]The universe of residential single-unit policies includes only those policies purchased for a single unit.

[22]To calculate these proportions, the universe is all residential policies and includes single units as well as all condominium policies.

[23]We used claims data as presented in BureauNet available through March 31, 2013, to calculate the average residential and commercial claim amounts. The yearly claims data were adjusted for inflation before the average was calculated.

nationwide averages, areas with very little flooding may mask areas with heavier flooding and bring the national average down.

Figure 1: Change in Proportion of Residential and Commercial Policies at Maximum Building Coverage, 2002 through 2012

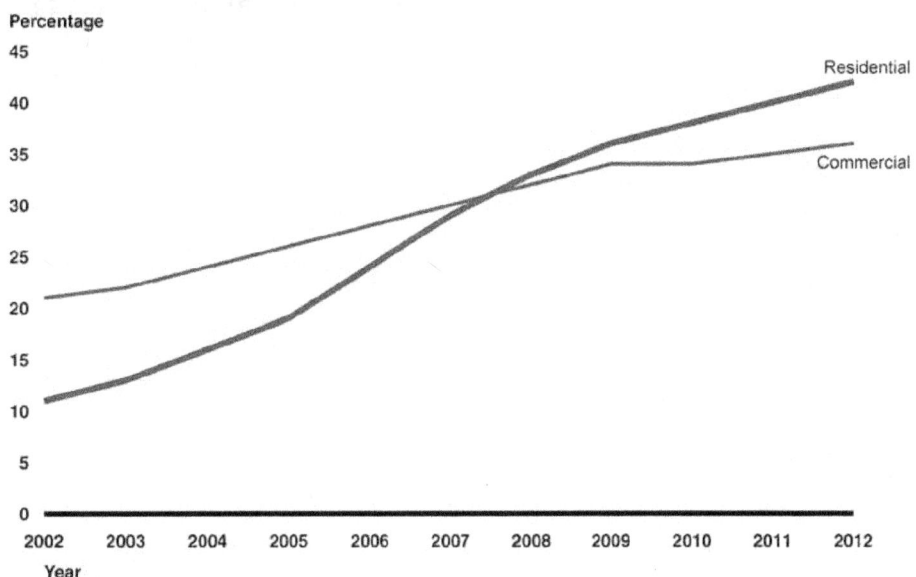

Source: GAO analysis of NFIP's database of policies.

We analyzed the number of NFIP residential single-unit policyholders by state as of September 30, 2011, to determine which states had the highest number of these policyholders with maximum building coverage (see fig. 2). Based on our analysis, just over half of all NFIP policies and about 25 percent of all residential single-unit policies at maximum coverage limits were from three Gulf Coast states: Florida, Texas, and Louisiana. Seven states—mostly located on the Gulf Coast and the Eastern Coast—made up 75 percent of all residential single-unit policyholders with maximum building coverage and about 35 percent of all residential single-unit policies. In comparing maximum coverage rates in individual states, we found that, in general, states with higher median home values also had a higher percentage of policyholders purchasing coverage at the maximum limit. For example, as shown in figure 2, the 2011 median home value in California was $355,600, and 63.5 percent of its policyholders purchased the maximum amount of NFIP building coverage. Similarly, in 2011 New York had a median home value of $285,300 and 65 percent of its residential single-unit policyholders purchased the maximum building coverage, the highest percentage of all 50 states. In contrast, West Virginia had the lowest median home value of $99,300, and about 7 percent of its policyholders purchased maximum building coverage, the lowest percentage of all the states. The national median home value as of September 2011 was $213,300, slightly below NFIP's current maximum coverage limit of $250,000 (buildings only).

Figure 2: Comparison of Median Home Values and Number and Percentage of Residential Single-Unit NFIP Policies at Maximum Building Coverage by State, 2011

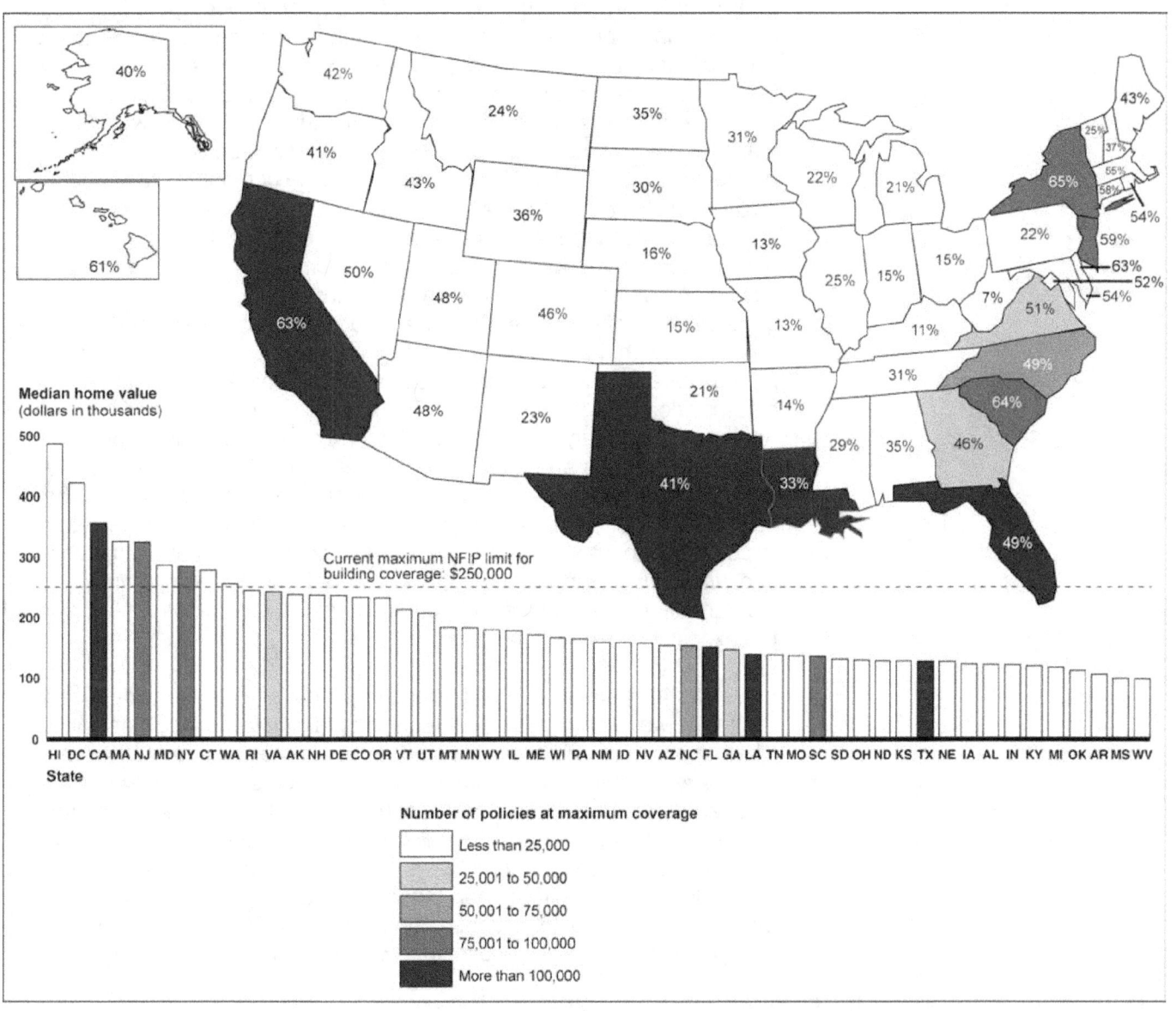

Sources: GAO analysis of NFIP's Database of Policies and American Community Survey data; Map Resources (map).

Notes: We excluded American Samoa, Guam, Puerto Rico, and Virgin Islands from our study because our analysis focused on states. In addition, because 2011 was the most recently available data for median home values through the American Community Survey, we used fiscal year 2011 NFIP data for this analysis.

GAO-13-568 Flood Insurance Coverage

Some policyholders may wish to purchase more flood insurance than is available through FEMA, but insurers are selective about providing this additional coverage, and it can be costly. Although aggregate information is not available on the precise size of the private flood insurance markets for residential and commercial properties, some brokers and other staff from industry organizations told us these markets are generally considered small. According to an industry survey and our own research, it appears that about 30 companies offer excess flood coverage to residential and commercial customers.[24] Some companies only serve residential clients, and some only serve commercial clients. Companies that participate in the excess insurance market are selective about the risk levels they are willing to insure. Some brokers, insurers, and staff at industry organizations we talked to said that insurance companies generally only offer residential excess flood insurance to owners of high-value homes that are well constructed, up to code, and not located in high-risk areas, such as those designated as Zone A or V (high-risk and high-risk coastal). For example, one insurer said that it insures high-value homes with coverage up to $15 million and that the average value of the homes it insures is about four to five times higher than the average value of homes that NFIP insures. Similarly, on the commercial side, another insurer said that it only made flood coverage available to gain or retain an important account, rather than because of an interest in providing private flood insurance. Further, the company stated that it does not write insurance for small businesses, primarily due to the catastrophic nature of the exposure presented by floods.

Industry stakeholders told us that the high cost of excess residential flood insurance was another factor influencing policyholders' decisions about whether or not to purchase this coverage, but precise information on the costs was difficult to obtain. Insurers we contacted generally were reluctant to provide specific information on their rates because the rates are based on many variables unique to each home and are therefore not generalizable. Three common variables used to determine rates are flood zone, elevation of building, and the value of the home. However, staff from insurance industry organizations told us that not many residential policyholders purchase excess flood coverage because of its high price.

---

[24]The number of companies offering excess flood insurance coverage may be higher or lower as insurance companies are constantly entering and exiting the market and because the industry survey and our research may have overlooked some companies offering this type of coverage.

For example, one broker told us that the starting point for an excess flood rate he had negotiated before Superstorm Sandy was about $.3125 for every $100 of insurance on building coverage for a post-FIRM property built in a high-risk area (Zone A) that had been built to the required base flood elevation.[25] Based on this rate, $500,000 in excess flood coverage on a building would cost approximately $1,562 annually. However, the broker also indicated that other variables would change the rate so that the costs for excess flood insurance on this property could range from $1,200 to $3,000. According to www.floodsmart.gov, a website about NFIP maintained by FEMA, NFIP's average insurance policy costs about $600 per year, but the rates vary substantially between zones and can range from $412 for a preferred risk policy for maximum coverage for the building and contents in Zones B, C, or X (moderate to low risk) to $4,375 for a pre-FIRM standard policy for a primary residence in a high-risk coastal area (Zone V) with maximum building coverage.[26] One insurance company official told us that they charged twice NFIP's additional rate for properties in the same zone.[27] Insurers and brokers that we talked to explained that many variables affect the rate charged, and these factors vary for each property. One broker explained that the rating sheet he used to determine quotes to consumers was 30 pages.

Excess flood insurance coverage for commercial policies can be similarly restrictive and costly. For example, one insurer explained that costs varied for excess coverage depending on the flood zone where the property was located. For every $100 of total insurable value, the cost for buildings in Zone A (high-risk) would range from 5 cents to 50 cents, and the cost in Zones B or C (moderate to low risk) would range from half a cent to 10 cents. As a result, $5,000,000 in coverage could cost between

---

[25]The base flood elevation is the elevation relative to mean sea level at which there is a 1 percent chance of flood waters rising in a given year. The level of base flood elevation within a community can change throughout the floodplain. Pre-FIRM refers to a property that was built prior to the development of the community's Flood Insurance Rate Map (FIRM).

[26]Floodsmart.gov provides information about NFIP and types of flood coverage, as well as about flood risks and what causes floods.

[27]NFIP has two rates. The basic rate covers the first $60,000 of coverage, and the additional rate is for any insurance purchased above $60,000. According to NFIP's Flood Insurance Manual, revised May 2013, NFIP's additional rate can range from 25 cents for every $100 of coverage for a residential single-family building with no basement in a low-risk zone to $1.94 for the same structure type in a high-risk coastal zone. Rates vary based on a number of factors such as building type, occupancy, and zone.

$250 and $25,000 in annual premiums. However, this provider also said that the flood zone was only one factor used to determine pricing and that other factors and proprietary pricing also influenced these annual premiums. In addition to the factors listed for residential policies (i.e., flood zone, base flood elevation, and building value), insurers and brokers we interviewed said that premiums for commercial policies were also influenced by some or all of the following variables:

- proximity to Zones A (high risk) or B (moderate to low risk),
- whether the building has a basement,
- whether the building is built on a concrete slab,
- type of equipment located on the first floor,
- location of mechanical equipment,
- redundancy of operations (i.e., does the company have operations in another state or country that can continue the business), and
- whether the company has a disaster recovery plan in place.

In addition to high costs, staff at consumer advocacy organizations and insurance industry organizations described a number of other reasons that a consumer might decide not to purchase flood insurance in general. Some consumers are not sure whether they should purchase flood insurance, either because they think that a flood will never happen to them or because they are confused by the fact that it has to be purchased as a separate policy. Another reason that consumers choose not to purchase flood insurance is that they expect to get help through disaster relief efforts in the event of a catastrophe.

Raising NFIP's Coverage Limits Would Likely Increase Both Premiums Collected and the Program's Risk Exposure

Raising NFIP coverage limits would likely increase the program's risk exposure, particularly in catastrophic years, although it could make coverage more affordable for some consumers. Stakeholder opinions vary regarding the potential effects that raising coverage limits would have on the private insurance market and on consumers. Opinions also vary regarding the potential effects of lowering coverage limits.

Estimated Effect on NFIP of Raising or Lowering Its Coverage Limit

We estimated the potential financial effect on NFIP if coverage limits had been raised between 2002 and 2011 and found that higher coverage limits would have been associated with increased net revenue—

premiums less claim amounts—in most years. We estimated the impact on premiums, claim amounts, and net revenues for each fiscal year from 2002 through 2011 under various hypothetical scenarios in which the maximum building coverage limit for residential dwellings was $417,000— the conforming loan limit for Fannie Mae and Freddie Mac in 2006— instead of $250,000.[28] We limited our analysis to nonsubsidized residential policies.[29] We made a number of assumptions to conduct the analysis that likely result in overstating both the amount of additional premium revenue that would have been collected and the amount of additional claims.[30] To some extent these overstatements would offset each other in terms of their estimated impact on net revenues.

We first assumed a baseline scenario in which all of the policyholders with maximum building coverage from fiscal years 2002 through 2011 increased their coverage to the new maximum. Under this baseline scenario, we also assumed that all of these policyholders paid additional premiums at the same rate as for their coverage just below the $250,000 limit. In addition, we assumed that those policyholders who received the maximum building claim amount during the period examined also would have received an additional building claim amount of $167,000. We calculated the additional premiums that would have been paid by the policyholders, the additional claim amounts received by these policyholders, and the additional net revenue under these assumptions. Finally, we calculated the actual premiums, actual claim amounts, and actual net revenue for the policyholders with maximum coverage as benchmarks for comparison.

[28]As noted earlier, Fannie Mae and Freddie Mac are restricted by law to purchasing single-family mortgages with origination balances below a specific amount, known as the "conforming loan limit."

[29]Nonsubsidized policies accounted for about 70 percent of all residential policies at the end of fiscal year 2012. Our analysis excludes subsidized and commercial policies because they are rated differently.

[30]According to FEMA officials, the rate schedule might change if coverage limits were increased, thereby decreasing the amount of additional premiums collected. It is also possible that claims would not increase to the full extent of the increase in coverage. Further, our assumption that 100 percent of policyholders at the maximum coverage limit would have increased their coverage also likely overstates the percentage of policyholders who would do so, and excludes any potential antiselection as to which policyholders choose to increase their coverage.

Our results for this baseline scenario suggest that higher coverage limits would have been associated with increased net revenues in most fiscal years from 2002 through 2011. For all fiscal years except 2004 and 2005, our baseline estimates of additional premiums are greater than our estimates of additional claims. For fiscal years 2004 and 2005—years when the program experienced catastrophic losses—our estimates of additional premiums are less than our estimates of additional claim amounts, and the program would have been exposed to additional risk.[31] As noted in table 2, in most years premiums collected from all policies exceed claims paid, except for particularly catastrophic years. FEMA officials explained that most of the losses that NFIP covers are fairly small and usually fall below the current residential policy limits of $250,000 until a catastrophic event occurs, such as Hurricane Katrina. However, in addition to paying claims, NFIP premiums are also used to pay the costs associated with administering the program, such as WYO expenses, operating expenses, flood insurance studies, floodplain management, and FEMA administrative costs. Our analysis assumes that a higher coverage limit would not result in materially higher administrative expenses for the program.

Table 2: Baseline Estimated Impact of Higher Building Coverage Limits, Fiscal Years 2002-2011

Dollars in millions, not adjusted for inflation

Fiscal year	Benchmark			Baseline		
	Actual premiums	Actual claim amounts	Actual net revenue[a]	Estimated additional premiums	Estimated additional claim amounts	Estimated additional net revenue
2002	$563	$83	$480	$31	$0.2	$31
2003	584	178	406	36	3	34
2004	619	1,217	-598	44	71	-26
2005	658	6,058	-5,400	55	320	-265
2006	713	86	627	71	2	70
2007	752	88	665	87	2	84
2008	805	684	121	100	30	70
2009	822	142	679	107	4	103

[31]Fiscal years 2004 and 2005 were particularly catastrophic. For example, FEMA paid losses totaling $1.9 billion for four hurricanes that made landfall in August and September 2004. The following year, FEMA paid losses of $16 billion for two hurricanes that made landfall near the end of the fiscal year.

Dollars in millions, not adjusted for inflation

Fiscal year	Benchmark			Baseline		
	Actual premiums	Actual claim amounts	Actual net revenue[a]	Estimated additional premiums	Estimated additional claim amounts	Estimated additional net revenue
2010	899	120	780	105	4	101
2011	934	257	676	121	5	116

Source: GAO analysis of FEMA data.

Notes: We analyzed nonsubsidized policies on residential single-unit dwellings rated using the flood insurance manual effective as of September 30 of each year from 2002 through 2011. Maximum building coverage is $250,000 and the maximum building claim payment is also $250,000. Fiscal years are from October 1 of the previous year to September 30 of the following fiscal year. For our baseline estimates, we assumed that all of the policyholders in our sample with maximum building coverage increased their building coverage from $250,000 to $417,000 and paid additional premiums consistent with this additional coverage amount. We used the actual rates as reported in the NFIP policy data to estimate the additional premium amounts. We also assumed that these policyholders received additional building claim amounts of $167,000 ($417,000 minus $250,000) for any claims for which they received the maximum building claim payment. We calculated the additional premiums paid by the policyholders, the additional claim amounts received by these policyholders, and the additional net revenue based on these assumptions. We calculated the actual premiums paid by all policyholders in our sample, actual claims received by all policyholders in our sample, and actual net revenue from these policyholders as a benchmark for comparison. These figures were not adjusted for inflation. We do not sum the results because our analysis was based on a subset of the population and because of the number of assumptions in the analysis.

[a]Net revenue is prior to deductions for the program's administrative expenses.

We analyzed additional scenarios using variations in our assumptions and found similar results. We examined different combinations of (1) the increase in premiums being 20 percent lower than the baseline estimate; (2) the increase in claims being 20 percent lower than the baseline estimate; and (3) the percentage of policyholders increasing their coverage 25 percent, 50 percent, or 75 percent of all policyholders. As with the baseline scenario, the results from these additional scenarios all suggest that higher coverage limits would have been associated with increased net revenue in most of the years analyzed, except for the years with catastrophic losses. In these years, the scenario results show that net revenues would have been negative, exposing the program to additional losses. The estimated additional net revenue shown in table 2, both positive and negative, would be scaled down if fewer than 100 percent of policyholders at the $250,000 maximum chose to increase their coverage. See appendix I for details on these additional scenarios.

Our analysis suggests that the effect on the financial condition of the program of raising NFIP's coverage limits would depend on a number of factors. For example, the number and selection of policyholders who increase their coverage, the additional premiums they pay, and the additional amounts they receive for claims on their policies are all factors.

In particular, changes in the rate schedule of any additional coverage and consequent changes in coverage that policyholders make in response could change the impact of raising coverage limits on NFIP's financial condition. As stated earlier, FEMA charges a lower rate for coverage above $60,000. Although we assumed that the flood insurance rate schedule would remain constant, FEMA officials indicated that the rate schedule might decrease at higher coverage limits, and that our methodology likely overstates the increase in premiums as a result. Policyholders might respond to changes in the rate schedule by adjusting their coverage amounts. To the extent that coverage amounts change, claim amounts may change as well. We did not attempt to quantify the potential impact of these further changes.

Overall, the financial impact on the program of raising coverage limits would depend on the adequacy of the rates that would be charged for the additional coverage. If the size of the program and risk exposure were increased by raising coverage limits, setting rates for the additional coverage that accurately reflect the risk would be important, or the financial stability of the program would be undermined. FEMA officials said that as long as NFIP rates accurately reflect the actual risk of flooding, increasing the coverage limits should not affect the program because even though FEMA would occasionally pay out more with the increased limits, it would also be collecting more income from higher premiums, which would help offset the occasional increased payouts. However, in a 2009 report we raised concerns about FEMA's rate-setting process.[32] We found that the annual amount that NFIP collects in both full-risk and subsidized premiums is not enough to cover its operating costs, claim losses, and principal and interest payments for the debt owed to Treasury, thereby exposing the federal government and ultimately taxpayers to ever-greater financial risks, especially in years of catastrophic flooding. In addition, we recommended that FEMA ensure that its rate-setting methods result in rates that accurately reflect flood risks. As previously discussed, the Biggert-Waters Act requires FEMA to implement a number of changes to its rate-setting process, including eliminating certain subsidies; phasing out other subsidies and grandfathered policies; building a reserve fund; and updating maps that reflect the relevant information on topography, long-term erosion of shorelines, future changes in sea levels, and the intensity of hurricanes.

---

[32]GAO-09-12.

As of June 2013, FEMA's efforts to implement many of these reforms were ongoing.

Similarly, lowering NFIP coverage limits would lessen the program's risk exposure. A representative from one insurance industry organization also said that lowering coverage limits would take premiums away from the program and make it less structurally sound. However, FEMA officials stated that if coverage limits were lowered, they would adjust premium levels upward to account for the decreased income the program would receive. As of September 2012, about 28 percent of all residential single-unit policies were for less than $150,000 in coverage and about 48 percent of commercial policies had less than $350,000 in coverage.

Effect on the Private Flood Insurance Market of Raising or Lowering the Coverage Limit

Brokers and staff from insurance industry organizations told us that the private flood insurance market would have less risk exposure if NFIP were to raise its coverage limits because the point at which NFIP's coverage ended and their coverage began, called the "attachment point," would be higher. This would lessen the premiums collected and overall risk exposure of the private flood insurance market. For example, a home valued at $750,000 needs $500,000 in additional coverage based on the current coverage limits offered by NFIP. If NFIP's coverage limits were increased to $350,000, then the private excess market would only need to provide coverage for $400,000. Further, one insurer that we talked to said that NFIP's coverage limits should be raised because the value of homes has increased since the coverage limits last increased in 1994 to the current limits. According to FEMA officials, the prior building coverage limit was $185,000, set in 1977; thus the building coverage limits have increased about 35 percent in 36 years.

Staff from one insurance industry organization told us that increased NFIP coverage limits might push other insurers that currently provide flood insurance above NFIP's current limit of $250,000 out of the market. They explained that fewer companies would be needed because fewer people would need to purchase additional flood insurance coverage, as they might be able to get all the insurance they needed through NFIP. However, as discussed earlier, insurers and brokers noted that companies providing excess coverage tend to insure more expensive properties.

When we asked industry stakeholders about the potential effects of lowering coverage limits, staff from some industry organizations told us that insurers might drop out of the market due to increased risk and inability to compete with NFIP's lower premium rates. Overall, some industry stakeholders we talked to did not think that either raising or lowering NFIP's coverage limits would have a major effect on the excess flood insurance market.

Effect on Consumers of Raising or Lowering the Coverage Limit

Opinions varied on how NFIP raising coverage limits would affect consumer participation in the program. Although raising coverage limits would provide more coverage options for consumers, staff at consumer advocacy organizations and insurance industry organizations told us that raising coverage limits might have minimal impact on overall consumer participation. The general consensus was that consumers with homes valued higher than $250,000 would be interested in NFIP increasing its coverage limits and would likely purchase more coverage through NFIP if it were available. As we noted earlier, the percentage of residential and commercial policies at the maximum coverage amounts increased from 2002 through 2012, suggesting possible additional demand for increased coverage limits. However, these points are applicable to rates in place prior to the Biggert-Waters Act, and consumers' decisions may be different based on higher rates after the act's implementation.

One FEMA official said that raising the coverage limits could make premiums more affordable to consumers whose homes were valued at less than $250,000. He explained that if policyholders who currently buy the maximum amount of coverage also bought the increased coverage and paid the additional premiums, FEMA could lower its overall rates to reach the income level needed to covers its expenses, which would lower the rates for those who do not purchase the maximum coverage.[33] For example, if NFIP were to sell 40 percent more coverage on average, it could also expect to get 40 percent more premiums on average if it did not change the rates. Although total premiums collected might increase by 40 percent, the claims payouts would likely be more modest because smaller claim amounts are more common, and the entire increase in premiums would not be needed to cover losses. As a result, flood

[33]FEMA's model for setting rates incorporates data on flood risks generated by a hydrologic model that is based on largely the same principles as hazard risk models used by private insurers and other federal agencies. FEMA uses this rate model to generate prices for flood insurance according to estimates of flood risk and expected flood damage. It sets rates on a nationwide basis, combining and averaging across many geographically diverse areas.

insurance premiums for individual policyholders could be lowered to reach the required levels for the program. However, FEMA officials did not know specifically how rates might change if coverage limits were changed. Staff at one consumer advocacy organization and at one industry organization said that most consumers only purchase the amount they are required to purchase and would probably not purchase additional coverage if the limits were raised. As previously noted in figure 2, the median home value in the majority of states is below NFIP's current maximum building limit.

Alternatively, if NFIP were to lower its coverage limits, it could force more consumers whose homes are valued at greater than the limit to purchase insurance in the private excess flood market, to the extent it is available. If insurers in the excess flood market were not willing to lower their attachment point, it could create a gap in coverage between what the private insurance market was willing to offer and the new NFIP maximum coverage limit. Staff at some consumer advocacy and industry organizations said that lowering NFIP's coverage limits could increase the demand for excess insurance—either by homeowners' choice or by lenders forcing consumers to purchase additional flood insurance to cover the value of their homes. Others told us that it might not change consumer participation at all since most consumers only purchased what they were required to purchase.

Additional Options Could Expand Coverage for Some but Could Undermine NFIP's Financial Stability

Adding optional coverage for business interruption or additional living expenses could have both advantages and disadvantages for NFIP, the private market, and consumers. These optional types of coverage could potentially bring in some additional revenue to NFIP or expand the affordability and availability to customers, therefore lowering overall uninsured risk in the market. However, NFIP would need to make changes to its underwriting and claims processing to take into consideration the complexities associated with each type of coverage or its financial stability could be further undermined.

Coverage for Business Interruption

Adding business interruption coverage could offer several advantages for NFIP. To the extent that premiums for business interruption coverage reflect the actual risks, adding this type of coverage could result in additional revenue to the program. Some brokers we interviewed also said that adding business interruption coverage to NFIP could result in less uninsured risk in the market. Under the assumption that FEMA's rates would be lower than private market industry rates, industry stakeholders told us that more small- and medium-sized companies might be able to purchase this coverage because it would be more affordable to them. Further, large businesses might be inclined to buy more business interruption coverage. In general, more businesses buying coverage would result in less uninsured risk and could offset the need for some government disaster relief payments.

However, underwriting business interruption coverage and adjusting claims could be challenging for FEMA because it lacks needed expertise. We have previously found that underwriting this type of coverage is complex and that properly pricing the risk for business interruption coverage requires extensive evaluation of a company's business model and cash flow.[34] For example, an insurance broker told us that commercial customers typically are required to complete a two- to three-page financial worksheet providing historical information on net income and continuing expenses for the period to be insured, including costs such as payroll, rent, utilities, and other ongoing expenses that an owner would be expected to pay even if the building were destroyed. This information is used to determine the amount of coverage the insurer is willing to offer and the price of the coverage. Underwriting business interruption coverage is complex because predicting the costs associated with flood-related damage is difficult. An academic study noted that in order to predict the potential losses from a flood, insurers would need to consider not only the direct damage to a property but also the implications of a flood on the company's other locations, infrastructure, supply chains, and employees.[35] In addition to the complexities of underwriting, we have previously found that adjusting business interruption claims is also challenging because the extent of losses depends on the nature of the business and the circumstances surrounding the loss.[36] Further, one broker explained that the expertise of forensic accountants is necessary

---

[34]GAO, *Information on Proposed Changes to the National Flood Insurance Program*, GAO-09-420R (Washington, D.C.: Feb. 27, 2009).

[35]Adam Rose and Charles Huyck, "Improving Catastrophe Modeling for Business Interruption Insurance Needs" (paper presented at the National Bureau of Economic Research Conference on Insurance Markets and Catastrophe Risk, Cambridge, Mass.: May 12, 2012).

[36]GAO-09-420R.

to adjust for claims.[37] NFIP officials stated that they would need to hire additional experts such as lawyers, adjusters, and forensic accountants if they added business interruption coverage—experts with a deeper and more thorough understanding of underwriting and claims processing.

In addition to these challenges, if the rates NFIP charged for business interruption coverage were not adequately risk-based, adding such coverage could negatively impact the program's financial stability and thus further increase taxpayer exposure. Further, adverse selection could increase the program's risk if only those businesses with the highest risk or the highest claims purchased business interruption coverage from NFIP. Some insurers, brokers, and staff from industry organizations that we talked to emphasized the importance of careful underwriting of business interruption coverage because underestimating the potential costs can lead to losses for insurers. For example, one broker we interviewed explained that after Hurricane Katrina, some private insurers suffered losses from business interruption coverage because businesses were closed for such a long period that the losses from this coverage were greater than the actual value of the building that was damaged. Although FEMA officials told us that they planned to price any new coverage at a rate equivalent to the actual risk for flood, we have previously raised concerns about how FEMA's rates are calculated and suggested that the rate-setting process does not fully take into account all relevant factors.[38] Collectively, these factors increase the risk that full-risk premiums, as set by FEMA, on any new coverage may be insufficient to cover future losses, adding to concerns about NFIP's financial stability.

Adding business interruption coverage to NFIP could also have unintended consequences for private insurance companies. NFIP officials

---

[37]Forensic accounting is a specialty practice area of accountancy that provides evidence used to resolve disputes or litigation. This expertise is often needed in adjusting for business insurance claims as there are many variables that impact the estimate of the business income claim.

[38]See GAO-09-12. In this report we found that FEMA sets flood insurance rates on a nationwide basis, combining and averaging many topographic factors that are relevant to flood risk, so that these factors are not specifically accounted for in setting rates for individual properties. Some patterns in historical claims and premium data suggest that NFIP's rates may not accurately reflect differences in flood risk. We also found that FEMA does not fully take into account factors such as ongoing and planned development, long-term trends in erosion, or the effects of global climate change, although private-sector models are incorporating some of these factors.

told us that the availability of business interruption coverage in the private market is limited because few companies offer private flood insurance. According to one broker's estimate, about 10 or 12 insurance companies currently offer business interruption coverage for flooding. Some stakeholders suggested that similar to increasing coverage limits, adding this coverage to NFIP could provide a disincentive for private insurers to continue offering it. In addition, any change to the federal flood insurance program would create an increased burden on WYO insurers from an administrative and operations perspective, as they would likely need to develop new forms, promote a new product, and respond to the additional volume of work.

Optional coverage for business interruption through NFIP could potentially expand the affordability and availability of this coverage for certain commercial consumers. Business interruption coverage is expensive through the private market and is generally only purchased by large companies. For example, one insurance broker that we spoke with told us that although interest in coverage for business interruption from companies of all sizes is high, generally only larger companies can afford it. Staff from an industry association and an insurer further concurred that the high cost of business interruption coverage prevents small- and medium-sized companies from purchasing it. A representative from an industry organization testified that including business interruption coverage would help provide stability to local economies affected by flooding and could provide needed security to small businesses.[39] However, whether NFIP could offer business interruption coverage at premium rates that are affordable and still adequately risk-based is unclear.

Coverage for Additional Living Expenses

The potential impact on NFIP of offering coverage for additional living expenses could depend on how the coverage is structured. In 2009, FEMA contracted for a study that focused on NFIP offering additional living expense coverage.[40] According to the FEMA study, offering

---

[39]Spencer Houldin, Representative for the Independent Insurance Agents & Brokers of America, testimony before the House Committee on Financial Services, Subcommittee on Insurance and Housing, 112th Congress 1st session, March 11, 2011.

[40]Deloitte Consulting LLP, *Increasing the Scope of Coverage of the National Flood Insurance Program, Providing Coverage for Additional Living Expenses*, (McLean, Va.: July 10, 2009).

additional living expense coverage in the same way as private insurers—that is, to cover increases in expenses to maintain a household's normal standard of living—may not be the most appropriate option for NFIP, in part because it would be difficult to price. As with business interruption coverage, inadequate pricing for additional living expense coverage could further increase taxpayer exposure. In addition, similar to business interruption coverage, the program's risk could be further increased by adverse selection if only the homeowners at higher risk purchased the coverage.

The appropriate price of additional living expenses could be difficult for NFIP to determine. According to one insurer we interviewed, the premium rate for a standard homeowner's policy that includes additional living expenses for perils other than flood is based on historical losses, including historical losses from additional living expenses. However, FEMA does not have historical data on additional living expense losses for flood, and the usefulness of any data from private insurers that offer this coverage is limited because these policies typically cover only a specific subset of the market and may not account for the larger number of policyholders that NFIP would cover in a disaster-stricken area. The FEMA study noted that estimating the expected length of time policyholders would be displaced and expected costs of claims would be difficult. For example, in the case of widespread, catastrophic flooding, the time required to repair a property or relocate policyholders and the increased demand for a limited supply of temporary living arrangements could increase the payments NFIP would have to make.[41] Individuals were displaced for long periods of time following Hurricane Katrina. Because of the difficulty in estimating potential losses and determining adequate pricing, the risk exists that premiums collected may not cover losses, which could increase the government's exposure if FEMA needed to rely on its borrowing authority to cover any shortfall. The FEMA study concluded that if additional living expense coverage was offered through NFIP, a more basic structure that was easier to manage would be more appropriate. For example, the study suggested that offering a set dollar amount or a per diem rate for a specified period to help policyholders offset their additional expenses would be a better fit for NFIP, rather than

---

[41]FEMA officials said that if coverage for additional living expenses was not designed carefully, the coverage could result in competition with other disaster assistance and disaster recovery efforts following a catastrophic event by bidding up the costs for the limited housing available.

offering full coverage for a number of variables that might differ between homeowners. Although adding optional coverage for additional living expenses poses some of the same difficulties as business interruption coverage, FEMA officials explained that coverage for additional living expenses is much simpler to administer.

Adding living expense coverage could also have unintended consequences for private insurance companies. First, WYOs would need to adjust for changes in claims processing. For example, claims adjusters would need to conduct additional work to verify the damage to the property, the length of time the policyholder was displaced, and the policyholder's description of normal living expenses in order to avoid potential fraud or inflation of claims. In addition, staff at an industry organization told us that if NFIP were to begin offering coverage for additional living expenses but offered it at subsidized prices (i.e., prices that did not reflect the full risk), private companies that do offer this coverage could be priced out of the market. Also, staff at one industry organization stated that, similar to business interruption coverage, if FEMA were to begin offering optional coverage for additional living expenses WYO's would probably have to make administrative changes to their flood insurance and marketing programs.

Offering additional living expense coverage could provide more options for consumers, but few consumers might take advantage of it. Coverage for additional living expenses resulting from flooding is available on a limited basis through the private market, such as through optional additional coverage added to an excess flood insurance policy. For example, according to the FEMA study, this coverage can be added to some excess flood insurance policies, with limits from $7,500 up to $107,500. However, as stated earlier, the number of policyholders who purchase excess flood insurance coverage is generally low, and those who do purchase it are typically high-income individuals with properties located in low-risk areas. Because the excess market is generally selective, NFIP coverage for additional living expenses could allow additional consumers the ability to purchase this type of coverage, although FEMA officials noted that depending on how the coverage was structured, it could be fairly expensive. A representative of an industry organization also noted that if the additional coverage were to increase the price of the premium, consumers would not necessarily elect to purchase the additional coverage. In addition, a representative from one consumer advocacy organization said that few consumers might take advantage of the coverage because they expect the federal government to come in following a disaster to provide relief.

Agency Comments

We provided a draft of this report to FEMA within the Department of Homeland Security for their review and comment. The Department noted that it concurred with our prior recommendation directing FEMA to take steps to ensure that methods and data used to set NFIP rates result in premiums that accurately reflect the risk of losses from flooding.

Further, the letter stated that FEMA has already taken several actions toward implementing this recommendation, such as revising damage calculations for flooding events that only reach the foundation of the structure and performing a climate change study to assess the long-term impacts of climate change on all aspects of NFIP, including insurance pricing and grandfathering. The letter also stated that FEMA has other ongoing efforts, including analyzing water-depth probability curves for various flood zones; performing geospatial analyses to determine the extent of zone grandfathering; and piloting studies to determine structural flood risk information (structure elevation and flood depths for various return periods) using geospatial data from flood study and terrain models. FEMA's anticipated completion date is the end of fiscal year 2013.

We are sending copies of this report to the appropriate congressional committees and the Secretary of Homeland Security. In addition, the report is available at no charge on the GAO website at http://www.gao.gov.

If you or your staff have any questions regarding this report, please contact me at (202) 512-8678 or cackleya@gao.gov. Contact points for our Offices of Congressional Relations and Public Affairs may be found on the last page of this report. GAO staff who made major contributions to this report are listed in appendix III.

Alicia Puente Cackley
Director,
Financial Markets and
 Community Investment

Appendix I: Objectives, Scope, and Methodology

Our objectives were to examine (1) existing flood insurance coverage; (2) the potential effects on the National Flood Insurance Program's (NFIP) financial condition, the private insurance market, and consumers of raising or lowering NFIP coverage limits; and (3) the potential effects on NFIP's financial condition, the private insurance market, and consumers of allowing NFIP to offer optional coverage for business interruption and additional living expenses. For the purposes of this review, we analyzed flood insurance data obtained from the Federal Emergency Management Agency (FEMA), NFIP, brokers, and insurance companies that offer primary and excess flood insurance coverage.

To describe the existing flood insurance market, we obtained NFIP's Policy and Claims Masterfiles as of September 30, 2012, and June 30, 2012, respectively. We analyzed NFIP's database of policies, which contains information on policy type, coverage amounts, rates, and other variables used to calculate premiums. We identified all residential single-unit and commercial claims with maximum coverage at the end of fiscal year 2012. We also analyzed the data to determine trends. We computed the aggregate number of all residential policies and commercial policies with maximum coverage since 2002 and the annual rate of policies with maximum coverage. We further analyzed residential single-unit policy coverage for 2011 to investigate the association between the percentage of each state's policyholders with maximum coverage and a state's median home value. Even though NFIP provides coverage to American Samoa, Guam, Puerto Rico, and the Virgin Islands, we excluded these territories from our analysis because they are not U.S. states. We calculated average payments for residential and commercial claims that were closed and closed without payment for the period from 2007 through 2012 using data from FEMA's BureauNet.[1] We used the Gross Domestic Product deflator from the Bureau of Economic Analysis to adjust for inflation and express claims payment amounts for all years in 2012 dollars.

Using NFIP's policy and claims databases, we estimated the effect on NFIP's financial condition of raising coverage limits from $250,000 to $417,000 by estimating the impact on net revenue (premiums less claim payments) for single-family dwellings from 2002 through 2011. The upper

---

[1]We used FEMA's BureauNet because we did not have claims data for the whole fiscal year for 2012. BureauNet is the system that FEMA uses to collect, manage, and access its policy, claims, and policyholder data.

limit of $417,000 used in our analysis was required by the Biggert-Waters Flood Insurance Reform Act of 2012 (Biggert-Waters Act) and corresponds to the conforming loan limit for Fannie Mae and Freddie Mac (the enterprises). The enterprises are restricted by law to purchasing single-family mortgages with origination balances below a specific amount, known as the "conforming loan limit." The limit was increased to $417,000 in 2006 and remained at this level as of 2012. To assess the impact of increased building coverage limits on premiums collected from policyholders, claim amounts paid to policyholders, and net revenues to NFIP, we used data from FEMA, including data from snapshots of NFIP's policy database described above as of September 30 of each year from 2002 through 2011 and data from NFIP's claims database, which contains information on claim payments as of June 30, 2012.

For each fiscal year, we used observations on nonsubsidized policies that were effective between October 1 and September 30 of the fiscal year, that were for single-family dwellings and that were rated using the flood insurance manual. We also used data on claims associated with these policies. Table 3 shows descriptive statistics for the set of policies and claims we analyzed.

Table 3: Policies and Claims for Nonsubsidized, Manually-Rated Policies for Residential Single-Family Dwellings, 2002-2011

Fiscal year	Policies effective	Policies with building coverage	Policies with maximum building coverage	Claims	Claims with building claim payments	Claims with maximum building claim payments
2002	1,516,916	1,480,522	200,094	9,442	6,526	1
2003	1,509,355	1,476,869	234,551	14,546	10,742	15
2004	1,541,872	1,512,358	286,098	30,508	20,084	422
2005	1,575,138	1,547,550	360,587	94,510	64,475	1,913
2006	1,615,927	1,584,955	466,529	5,469	4,035	9
2007	1,604,077	1,574,351	543,456	4,641	3,459	13
2008	1,589,025	1,560,527	596,732	23,188	17,448	181
2009	1,558,411	1,531,287	631,368	8,438	6,637	26
2010	1,553,573	1,527,842	664,182	6,865	5,132	26
2011	1,530,956	1,506,472	691,324	15,712	11,882	29

Source: GAO analysis of FEMA data.

Notes: We analyzed nonsubsidized policies on residential single-family dwellings rated using the flood insurance manual effective as of September 30 of each year from 2002 through 2011. Multiple claims can be associated with a single policy. Maximum building coverage is $250,000 and the maximum building claim payment is also $250,000. Fiscal years are from October 1 of the previous year to September 30 of the following year. Although the data used in our analysis of the proportion of policies with maximum building coverage in figure 1 are through 2012, the claims data needed for this analysis were only available through 2011. In addition, the data for this table are a subset of the universe of all residential at the end of the fiscal year that was analyzed for figure 1.

We identified the policies in our analysis sample with the maximum building coverage of $250,000. We also identified the claims associated with these same policies that paid the maximum building claim payment of $250,000. We estimated the impact of a higher building coverage limit—$417,000 instead of $250,000—on premiums, claim amounts, and net revenues in seven different scenarios (see table 4). First, for our baseline scenario, we assumed that all policyholders with maximum building coverage increased their coverage from $250,000 to $417,000; that their premium rates per $100 of additional building coverage did not change; and that they received an additional $167,000 on any claim for which they received the maximum building claim payment. To assess the sensitivity of our results on the assumptions that the rates used to calculate additional premiums are unchanged and that claim amounts for claims with the maximum building claim payment increased by $167,000, we analyzed three alternative scenarios that differed from the baseline scenario by either reducing the rates used to calculate additional premiums by 20 percent, reducing the additional claim amounts by 20 percent, or both. Second, to assess the sensitivity of our results to the assumption that all policyholders with maximum building coverage increase their coverage from $250,000 to $417,000, we also analyzed three alternative scenarios that differed from the baseline scenario by reducing the number of policyholders who increased their building coverage to 25, 50, and 75 percent. In these scenarios, we used simulations that randomly selected the policyholders who increased their building coverage a large number of times and then calculated the average impact on premiums, claims amounts, and net revenues. Third and finally, we calculated the actual premiums, actual claims amounts, and actual net revenue as benchmarks for comparison.

Table 4: Estimated Impact of Higher Building Coverage Limits in Alternative Scenarios, Fiscal Years 2002-2011

Dollars in millions, not adjusted for inflation

Fiscal year	Baseline scenario	Premium rates reduced by 20%	Claim amounts reduced by 20%	Premium rates and claims reduced by 20%	25% of policy-holders with maximum coverage increase coverage	50% of policy-holders with maximum coverage increase coverage	75% of policy-holders with maximum coverage increase coverage
2002	$31	$25	$31	$25	$8	$16	$23
2003	34	26	34	27	8	17	25
2004	-26	-33	-10	-19	-6	-12	-18
2005	-265	-276	-201	-212	-66	-132	-199
2006	70	56	70	56	18	35	52
2007	84	67	85	68	21	42	64
2008	70	50	76	56	18	35	53
2009	103	82	104	82	26	52	77
2010	101	80	101	80	25	50	75
2011	116	92	117	93	29	58	87

Source: GAO analysis of FEMA data.

Notes: We analyzed nonsubsidized policies on residential single-unit dwellings rated using the flood insurance manual effective as of September 30 of each year from 2002 through 2011. Maximum building coverage is $250,000, so that the maximum building claim payment is also $250,000. Fiscal years are from October 1 of the previous year to September 30 of the following fiscal year. For our baseline estimates, we assumed that all of the policyholders in our sample with maximum building coverage increased their building coverage from $250,000 to $417,000 and paid additional premiums consistent with this additional coverage amount. We used the actual premium rates as reported in the NFIP policy data to estimate the additional premium amounts. We also assumed that these policyholders received additional building claim amounts of $167,000 ($417,000 minus $250,000) for any claims for which they received the maximum building claim payment. We calculated the additional premiums paid by the policyholders, the additional claim amounts received by these policyholders, and the additional net revenue based on these assumptions. For the alternative scenarios, we reduced the rates used to calculate additional premiums by 20 percent, reduced the additional claim amounts by 20 percent, reduced both the additional premiums and the additional claim amounts by 20 percent, and reduced the number of policyholders who increased their building coverage to 25, 50, and 75 percent.

To assess the reliability of the data in the policy and claims database, we examined the variables in the databases for missing values and for coding errors. We verified that there were not any duplicate observations on a policy in a fiscal year. We identified and dropped observations in the policy snapshots that could not be identified as either subsidized or nonsubsidized. We identified and dropped observations in the claims data with the date of loss earlier than the policy effective date. We verified that there is one claim for each policy for each date of loss. We assessed the extent to which the premium amount reported in the policy data was equal to the premium calculated using rates and other variables reported in the

data. Based on our assessment, we determined that the data in both
databases were sufficiently reliable for our purposes.

To further address the effects on the private insurance market, NFIP, and
consumers if NFIP were to change its coverage limits, or if NFIP were to
offer optional coverage for business interruption and additional living
expenses, we obtained some data in an industry survey last updated in
2010 pertaining to flood insurance programs outside NFIP that offered
private flood insurance, catastrophe insurance that included coverage for
flood, and other non-lender-placed and lender-placed flood coverage. The
survey data included limits, minimum premiums, general restrictions, and
other variables related to flood insurance coverage. We used the data to
examine high-level information on costs associated with buying excess
flood insurance and geographic coverage, and we identified some
companies that offer coverage for business interruption or additional living
expenses. We verified this information to the extent possible with various
insurance companies listed and Internet research to ensure its accuracy
and determined that it was sufficiently reliable for the purposes of this
report. In addition, we interviewed industry experts, including officials from
FEMA, officials and representatives from five insurance associations, two
consumer advocacy groups, six insurance companies, and four brokers.
We selected insurance companies based on work conducted for a prior
report, suggestions from insurance industry officials, and Internet
research.[2] To address all objectives, we also reviewed our prior reports
and testimonies on flood insurance, and relevant studies conducted by
RAND Corporation, Wharton Risk Management and Decision Processes
Center, Deloitte Consulting LLP, the Congressional Research Service,
and academia.

We conducted this performance audit from September 2012 to July 2013
in accordance with generally accepted government auditing standards.
Those standards require that we plan and perform the audit to obtain
sufficient, appropriate evidence to provide a reasonable basis for our
findings and conclusions based on our audit objectives. We believe that
the evidence obtained provides a reasonable basis for our findings and
conclusions based on our audit objectives.

---

[2]GAO-09-420R.

Appendix II: Comments from the Department of Homeland Security

U.S. Department of Homeland Security
Washington, DC 20528

Homeland Security

June 19, 2013

Alicia Puente Cackley
Director, Financial Markets and Community Investment
U.S. Government Accountability Office
441 G Street, NW
Washington, DC 20548

Re: Draft Report GAO-13-568, "FLOOD INSURANCE: Implications of Changing Coverage
Limits and Expanding Coverage"

Dear Ms. Cackley:

Thank you for the opportunity to review and comment on this draft report. The U.S. Department
of Homeland Security appreciates the U.S. Government Accountability Office's (GAO's) work
in planning and conducting its review and issuing this report.

The Federal Emergency Management Agency (FEMA) recognizes that the National Flood
Insurance Program (NFIP) may be the only source of insurance against flood damage for many
residents in flood-prone areas. FEMA appreciates GAO's efforts in analyzing the NFIP database
of policies and claims, researching and reviewing relevant studies conducted by private industry,
and conducting numerous interviews with insurance experts, including representatives from
FEMA staff and consumer advocacy organizations to complete this report.

The draft report did not contain any new recommendations, but it did reference a prior GAO
recommendation[1], with which the Department concurred. Specifically, GAO recommended that
the Secretary of Homeland Security direct FEMA to take steps to ensure that the methods and
data used to set NFIP rates result in premiums that accurately reflect the risk of losses from
flooding.

FEMA Federal Insurance and Mitigation Administration Strategic Planning and Analysis
division personnel are working to implement this recommendation. FEMA has already:

- Revised damage calculations for flooding events that only reach the foundation of the
  structure;

- Re-assessed the current practice of nationwide average premiums over a variety of
  topographies and decided the administrative advantages merit its continuation for
  elevated structures; and

---

[1] GAO, *FLOOD INSURANCE: FEMA's Rate-Setting Process Warrants Attention*, GAO-09-12 (Washington, D.C.:
October. 31, 2008)

- Performed a climate change study to assess the long-term impacts of climate change on all aspects of the NFIP, including insurance pricing and grandfathering.

FEMA's current efforts to address the issues raised by GAO include:

- Analyzing water-depth probability curves for the various numbered flood zones (A01-A30 and V01-V30);

- Performing geospatial analyses to determine the extent of zone grandfathering; and

- Piloting studies to determine structural flood risk information (structure elevation and flood depths for various return periods) using geospatial data from flood study and terrain models.

FEMA's "Estimated Completion Date" for closing this recommendation with GAO is September 30, 2013.

Again, thank you for the opportunity to review and comment on this draft report. Please feel free to contact me if you have any questions. We look forward to working with you in the future.

Sincerely,

Jim H. Crumpacker
Director
Departmental GAO-OIG Liaison Office

2

Appendix III: GAO Contact and Staff Acknowledgments

GAO Contact	Alicia Puente Cackley, (202)512-8678 or cackleya@gao.gov
Staff Acknowledgments	In addition to the contact named above, Jill Naamane and Patrick Ward (Assistant Directors); William Chatlos, Christopher Forys, Courtney LaFountain, Jacquelyn Hamilton, Karen Jarzynka-Hernandez, Marc Molino, Rhonda Rose, Jennifer Schwartz, Frank Todisco, and Carrie Watkins made key contributions to this report.

GAO's Mission	The Government Accountability Office, the audit, evaluation, and investigative arm of Congress, exists to support Congress in meeting its constitutional responsibilities and to help improve the performance and accountability of the federal government for the American people. GAO examines the use of public funds; evaluates federal programs and policies; and provides analyses, recommendations, and other assistance to help Congress make informed oversight, policy, and funding decisions. GAO's commitment to good government is reflected in its core values of accountability, integrity, and reliability.
Obtaining Copies of GAO Reports and Testimony	The fastest and easiest way to obtain copies of GAO documents at no cost is through GAO's website (http://www.gao.gov). Each weekday afternoon, GAO posts on its website newly released reports, testimony, and correspondence. To have GAO e-mail you a list of newly posted products, go to http://www.gao.gov and select "E-mail Updates."
Order by Phone	The price of each GAO publication reflects GAO's actual cost of production and distribution and depends on the number of pages in the publication and whether the publication is printed in color or black and white. Pricing and ordering information is posted on GAO's website, http://www.gao.gov/ordering.htm. Place orders by calling (202) 512-6000, toll free (866) 801-7077, or TDD (202) 512-2537. Orders may be paid for using American Express, Discover Card, MasterCard, Visa, check, or money order. Call for additional information.
Connect with GAO	Connect with GAO on Facebook, Flickr, Twitter, and YouTube. Subscribe to our RSS Feeds or E-mail Updates. Listen to our Podcasts. Visit GAO on the web at www.gao.gov.
To Report Fraud, Waste, and Abuse in Federal Programs	Contact: Website: http://www.gao.gov/fraudnet/fraudnet.htm E-mail: fraudnet@gao.gov Automated answering system: (800) 424-5454 or (202) 512-7470
Congressional Relations	Katherine Siggerud, Managing Director, siggerudk@gao.gov, (202) 512-4400, U.S. Government Accountability Office, 441 G Street NW, Room 7125, Washington, DC 20548
Public Affairs	Chuck Young, Managing Director, youngc1@gao.gov, (202) 512-4800 U.S. Government Accountability Office, 441 G Street NW, Room 7149 Washington, DC 20548

Please Print on Recycled Paper.

www.ingramcontent.com/pod-product-compliance
Lightning Source LLC
Chambersburg PA
CBHW080629290526
45790CB00007B/2989